SWIMMING BASICS

C. Rob Orr and Jane B. Tyler

Illustrated by
Bill Gow

Photographs by
Emmett Wilson, Jr.

Created and Produced by
Arvid Knudsen

PRENTICE-HALL, Inc.
Englewood Cliffs, New Jersey

We dedicate this book
with all our love
to our parents.

*Special thanks to Jeffrey Barton, Brent Matheson,
Mark Matheson, Laurie Jean Matheson, Kurt
Matheson, David Knudsen and little Miss Hagen who
helped us with the photographs you see in this book.*

Book design by Arvid Knudsen

Printed in the United States of America

Prentice-Hall International, Inc., London
Prentice-Hall of Australia, Pty. Ltd., North Sydney
Prentice-Hall of Canada, Ltd., Toronto
Prentice-Hall of India Private Ltd., New Delhi
Prentice-Hall of Japan, Inc., Tokyo
Prentice-Hall of Southeast Asia Pte. Ltd., Singapore
Whitehall Books Limited, Wellington, New Zealand

10 9 8 7 6 5 4 3 2 1

Library of Congress Cataloging in Publication Data

Orr, Ron.
  Swimming basics.

  Includes index.
  SUMMARY: Text and illustrations introduce the fundamentals of competitive swimming with emphasis on different types of strokes and breathing techniques.
    1. Swimming—Juvenile literature.
[1. Swimming] I. Tyler, Jane B. joint author. II. Title.
GV837.6.O77   797.2'1   80-10474
ISBN 0-13-879601-7

CONTENTS

Introduction

Here is a clear, concise and simplified book for the person interested in competitive swimming. Rob Orr and Jane B. Tyler have brought their advanced knowledge to the introductory level, and their book gives the beginning swimmer sound instruction and advice.

Swimming is our nation's most popular activity, and U. S. Swimming is the governing body for all competitive swimming in this country, serving all levels of ability and all organizations.

We hope that the readers of this book will find swimming an enjoyable activity and perhaps will involve themselves actively in the many programs sponsored throughout this country by United States Swimming.

Any further questions you may have concerning competitive swimming in the United States should be directed to the national headquarters of United States Swimming, 3400 West 86th Street, Indianapolis, Indiana 46268.

Ray Essick, *Head Administrator*
United States Swimming

COME ON IN, THE WATER IS FINE!

6

1

SWIMMING

People have been swimming since the beginning of time. The thousands-of-years-old, ancient artworks of the Egyptians, Assyrians, Greeks and Romans illustrate men and women swimming in the water. The strokes that they used are quite recognizable. But the first book on swimming only appeared some 400 years ago in Germany. It is only since that time that swimming has tended to become more scientific. Swimming techniques have improved enormously since then, and we continue today to refine, develop and improve our swimming abilities.

Swimming is the most popular recreational activity in the United States. While water sports and activities are enjoyable to almost everyone, it is for that reason we should know how to swim correctly and efficiently. It is then safe and much more fun.

No one, let's repeat, no one should ever decide for himself or herself to jump off the side of a pool or a three meter-diving board into twelve feet of water without having had any sort of basic swimming or diving lessons. That is trouble! There are numerous things that should be learned before you go into the water.

We strongly recommend that you take advantage of the learn-to-swim programs offered by the Red Cross, YMCAs, YWCAs, YM-YWHAs, Boy Scouts of America, Girl Scouts of America, and/or other local organizations. Good swimming techniques and habits are best learned under the expert guidance of qualified instructors and coaches.

The learning process should be a gradual progression from one stroke to the next, quite possibly starting from the dog paddle and back float and proceeding on to more advanced stages of each, namely, the freestyle and the backstroke. As the beginner swimmer progresses on to intermediate and then advanced swimmer, he or she will be able to learn more strokes. The trudgen crawl, the sidestroke, the breaststroke, the backstroke, the butterfly, the freestyle, the elementary backstroke, the overarm sidestroke and the inverted breaststroke are among some of the skills an advanced swimmer can learn.

The following chapters are designed to demonstrate the four basic strokes used in competitive swimming. Whether you are a beginner, an intermediate or an advanced swimmer, mastery of these strokes is essential. The four are: freestyle, breaststroke, backstroke and butterfly. You must also learn about water safety, starts, turns and competitive swimming. Whether or not you choose to compete, we certainly hope our basic introduction to swimming will make you more aware of its benefits. At the same time, we hope you become involved in one or more of the many areas of swimming and aquatic sports that are both interesting and fun for you.

O.K. Let's start.

2

THE FREESTYLE OR CRAWLSTROKE

The freestyle, or crawlstroke, is the fastest of all the strokes. It is the most popular stroke used in recreational and competitive swimming. For a thorough understanding of it, let us break our freestyle (or crawlstroke) into the following four stages:

The areas of concentration will be:

1. Body position
2. Leg movement
3. Arm movement
4. Breathing and coordination.

It is very important that you acquire some previous swimming skills before undertaking the following strokes.

Body Position—"Float like a Log"

In the freestyle or crawl, the body position of the swimmer is in a front-prone, horizontal position, arms fully extended directly overhead, "floating like a log." The water line on your head is just above the eyebrows. The entire body is as flat as possible in the water. This will vary with each individual depending on his or her buoyancy.

Leg Movement—"Hip Flutter"

The kick is normally called the flutter kick, as the legs alternately flutter up and down. Let's start the kick at the hip and continue it all the way down to the toes. The knee and ankle do not bend a great deal; it is more of a relaxed bend. It is important to make sure you do not "shake" the leg, but kick each leg alternately, from the hip. The toes should naturally have a tendency to point in towards one another. The flutter kick aids in the forward progress of the swimmer. But it primarily helps to balance and stabilize the rotating body and the swinging action of the arms. It is quite similar to the movement of your free swinging arms as you walk.

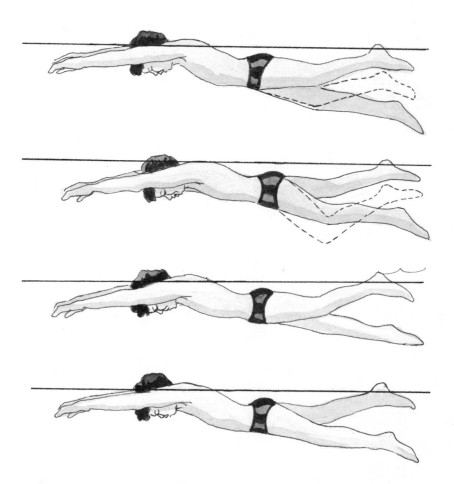

Arm Movement—"Catch, Grab, Pull, Push"

For you to start the arm movement, your body should be in the front-prone "log float," with both arms extended above the head. The work phase, or the pull, is begun with either one of the arms doing a downward and backward "catch" of the hand. The other arm remains extended above your head.

There are four stages of the arm pull:

1. Catch
2. Grab
3. Pull
4. Push

The *catch* of the hand is done with the palm facing towards the feet, *grabbing* down and back along an imaginary plane through the midline of the body, keeping the elbows up. As you continue with this freestyle arm movement the bent arm *pulls* past the shoulders and then *pushes* water directly back until the arm is at full extension with the thumb in a position to touch the thigh.

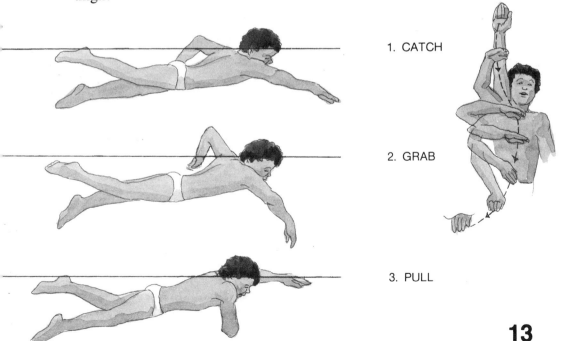

1. CATCH

2. GRAB

3. PULL

13

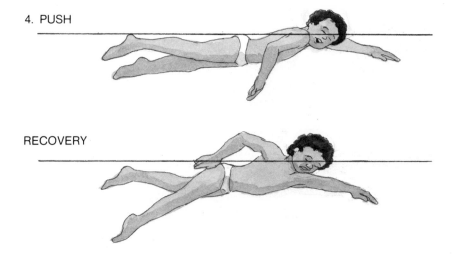

4. PUSH

RECOVERY

At this stage, after the first arm pull is complete, you will notice that your arms are constantly opposite one another, very similar to a windmill. One arm is still extended above your head in the "log float" position, while the opposite arm is extended down by your side.

The stroke is a nonstop movement with the recovery, or relax, phase of the stroke taking place immediately after the arm is fully extended to the side. At this moment the arm starts the recovery by lifting the elbow out of the water. At the same time, the other arm, still extended over the head, begins its catch phase of the stroke.

As the recovery arm is taken out of the water it is important to maintain a high elbow, with a relaxed hand over the water surface. The upper body will be rolling due to the arm action, allowing for an easy and relaxed recovery.

The entry of the recovery arm begins with the lower arm and hand slicing the water. finger tips first, about shoulder width, and stretching to full extension, getting ready to begin the next arm pull.

14

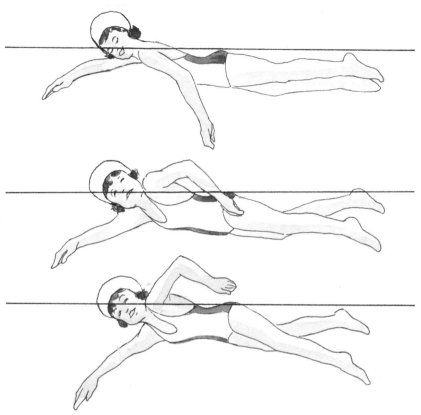

Breathing and Coordination

The breath is taken by rotating, not lifting, the head to the side just enough to clear the mouth above the water level. It should be taken just as the arm on the breathing side gets ready to start its recovery. Then after a quick breath the head is rotated back to its eyebrow position, approximately at the same time the recovery is completed. Before each breath is taken, you should exhale through your mouth and nose, prior to rotating your head. Each swimmer will have his or her preference as to which side to breathe on.

The leg movement usually results in a six-beat kick which means there are three downbeat kicks to the pull of one arm.

Variations on the kicking and breathing pattern are not uncommon among swimmers. It should be noted that one has to adapt to what works best for his or her individual form.

15

3

THE BACKSTROKE

The backstroke is a favorite stroke for both competitive and recreational swimmers. Our teaching experience has shown that beginning swimmers feel more comfortable learning backstroke than learning freestyle, breaststroke or butterfly. This is because the swimmer's face is out of the water. When swimming on the back, it is not only easier to breathe, but it is also easier to open the eyes. There is one problem however; unless you have eyes in the back of your head, you cannot see where you are going.

Let us break the backstroke into four basic parts:

1. Body position
2. Leg movement
3. Arm movement
4. Breathing and coordination

Before trying to swim the backstroke, we strongly suggest that a person first learn to float on the back, feeling completely relaxed.

Body Position—"Relax and float, letting the water hold the body up."

Correct body position in backstroke is very important. The swimmer should be flat on his back with the hips close to the surface of the water, the head lying back, and the water lining up at the ears. Remember to keep the back slightly arched with the hips up to avoid "sitting in the water." The head should stay fairly still with the eyes focusing on something directly in line with the body.

Leg Movement—"Boiling the Water"

A steady flutter kick is an important key to success. During the leg movement, the knees should bend slightly while the toes kick up. Also, the toes must be pointed with the ankles as loose as possible. The swimmer should think of "boiling water" with the toes, making very little splash.

Arm Movement

The little finger enters the water first, just behind or outside the shoulder. We can also say that the hands enter the water in the eleven o'clock and one o'clock positions with the palms facing away from the body. At this point, the hands drive down into the water 4 to 6 inches before starting to pull. The swimmer then pulls and pushes the water with a throwing motion. A simple way of describing the hand pattern is to say that it is a *down-up-down* movement. In other words, the water is thrown directly toward the feet with the palm of the hand. At the finish of the stroke, the hand is close to the leg and the palm faces the bottom of the pool.

After the push phase of the stroke, the hand is lifted out of the water. This is called the *recovery*. The easiest way to recover the arm is to keep it straight and to lift straight up. When the hand has traveled to its highest point in the air, the palm should be turned away from the body. This will make the little-finger entry possible.

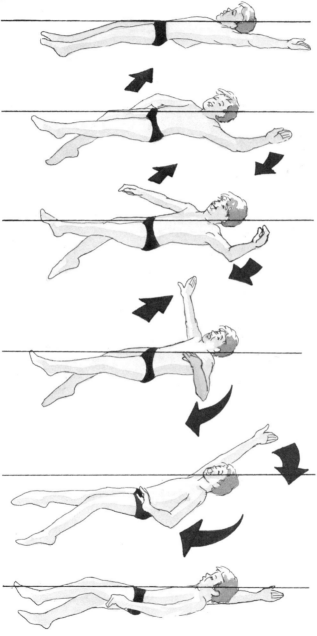

Breathing and Coordination

Now that we know how to move the arms and legs separately, let us see how we can swim the entire stroke in a relaxed and comfortable way. First, the hands must always be opposite each other. As one hand finishes pushing the water, the other hand must enter the water. At the same time, the toes must stay up and "boil" the water. Finally, we must have a simple breathing pattern. One simple pattern is to *breathe in* when the right hand comes out of the water and to *blow out* when the left hand comes out of the water. It is easiest to practice the breathing when the arms move at a slow, steady speed. It may take a little time to learn the breathing pattern, but once you do, the stroke will be much easier to perform.

4

THE BREASTSTROKE

The breaststroke, the slowest of the four strokes, is also the most unique. This can be seen in three ways. First, it is the only stroke in which the arms and legs remain under water. Second, it is the only stroke in which the legs are just as important as the arms in moving the swimmer forward. And third, it is one of the few strokes that allows the swimmer to see in front of himself while swimming.

When swimming breaststroke, it is easy to keep the head above water and to see where you are going. This is one reason breaststroke is used in lifesaving rescues. You might also see ladies at the local swim club swimming laps of breaststroke with their heads out of the water. But the only things they are trying to save are their new hair permanents and fresh make-up. We recommend, however, that you get the face wet when learning the stroke.

While the arm, leg, and head *(breathing)* movements are not difficult to learn alone, their coordination requires practice. Let us look first at how the various parts of the stroke are performed. We will then see how the parts can be put together to form the whole stroke.

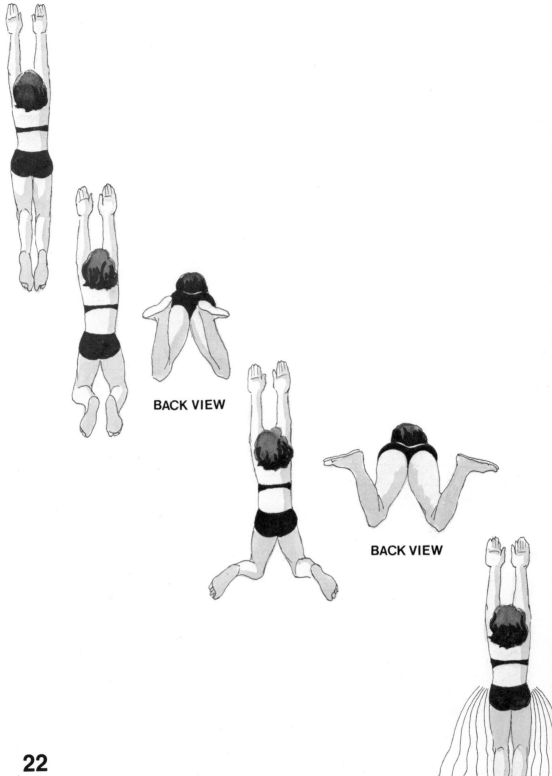

BACK VIEW

BACK VIEW

22

Body Position

Before the stroke begins, the body is stretched out on its front. The arms and hands reach forward while the legs and feet extend backward together. The hands should be four to six inches under water. The feet should be a little lower than the hands so that the body is at a slight angle in the water. At the same time the water should be at eyebrow level as the eyes focus on the hands. Finally, the head should remain in one position with the chin pushed forward.

Arm Pull

The breaststroke arm pull begins with the arms reaching forward with the hands four to six inches under water. The palms then press out, down, and back until the hands move to a point just outside the elbows. The hands then move inward and come together in *front* of the chin. At this point the hands shoot forward together until the arms are extended. A look at the diagram shows the pull is like an upside-down heart. Try to imagine drawing the heart with your fingertips as you press out, down, and back.

Remember: The pull is one smooth movement. The hands do not slow down as you pull. You should try to make your hands move faster as they "draw the heart."

Leg Movement

At the start of the breaststroke kick, the legs are extended six inches below the surface of the water. The heels are first picked up, then drawn up together into the fanny. The toes are turned out to the sides, keeping the knees inside the heels. The feet kick around and back together with the inside of the feet feeling the water. It is important to remember that if you kick the feet together each time, then the heels can come up together.

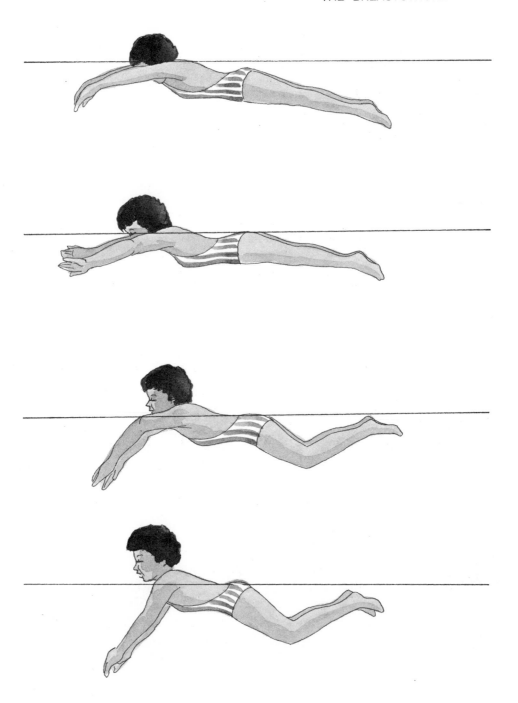

24

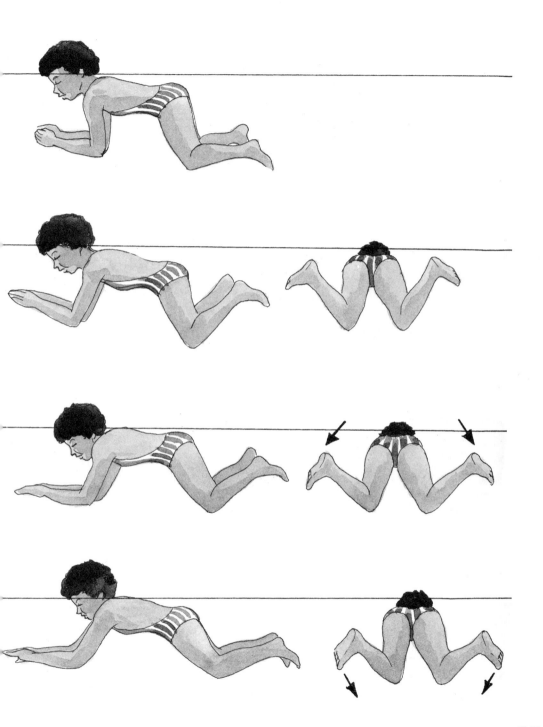

Breathing and Coordination

In breaststroke the breathing has much control over the timing of the arms and legs. A breath is taken in the middle of every stroke. The swimmer is to inhale quickly with the hands about halfway through the pull as the upper body comes out of the water. As the hands circle in underneath the body, the head is lowered to eyebrow level, making the body lunge forward. At this point, the breath is blown out. It must be made clear that the breathing must be smooth and controlled to avoid any unneeded pauses that might change the body position. At the end of the stretch, there may be a slight pause. This allows the legs to finish out the kick. When the arms are not pulling, the legs should be kicking.

5

THE BUTTERFLY STROKE

The butterfly stroke has just recently become the newest of the racing strokes. Swimming the butterfly requires a great deal of strength, rhythm, and coordination.

We have always liked swimming this stroke because it reminded us of a school of dolphins swimming in the ocean. In fact, the kick in the stroke is called just that, a dolphin kick. Once you have accomplished the skill of swimming this stroke, you will know that you have the makings of a competitive swimmer.

Body Position—"Float like a Log"

Similar to your freestyle-starting, floating position, the butterfly starts off in the same way. You should be in a front-prone horizontal position, your arms fully extended directly overhead, "floating like a log." The water line on your head is just above the eyebrows. The entire body is as flat as possible in the water.

Leg Movement—"Dolphin Kick"

The action of the legs is very similar to the way a dolphin kicks his tail to propel itself through the water. For this reason, the butterfly leg movement is called the dolphin kick.

It is performed in the same manner as the "hip flutter" kick in the freestyle with the exception that both legs act together in the kicking motion. Body rhythm is very important in doing the kick correctly.

Let us start the leg movement by lifting the hips and flexing both legs. This slight bending of the knees brings your heels up towards the surface of the water. Next we drop the hips and then straighten the legs and kick them to full extension, pointing the toes at the finish of the kick. Continuous application of the body and leg movements is very important in doing a correct butterfly stroke.

1. CATCH

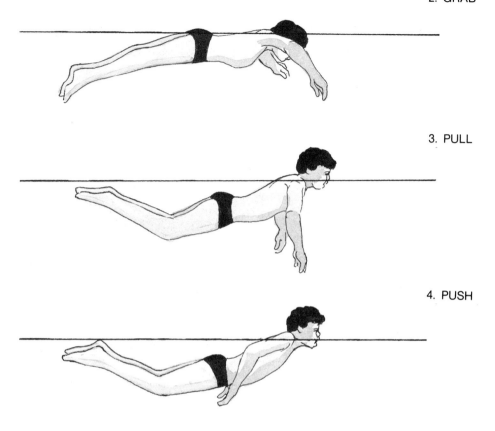

2. GRAB

3. PULL

4. PUSH

Arm Movement—"Catch, Grab, Pull, Push"

We must start the arm movement with both arms in the overhead extended position. The arms in the butterfly stroke work together in a motion similar to the freestyle pull. The difference you will find is that the swimmer doing the butterfly will not be able to roll on his or her side to assist in the breathing.

The "catch" is started by the palms of your outstretched hands facing downwards at shoulder width. The hands then slide to the side and downwards to "catch" the water. Without paus-

29

ing, the wrists and elbows bend slightly and ''grab'' the water. Keeping the elbows up, you ''pull'' your arms backwards down the midline of your body. Let us do the pull as if your arms and body were rolling over a barrel. As you finish rolling over the barrel your arms go into the ''push'' or full-extension position, placing your hands by your thighs.

The recovery begins by relaxing the wrists and raising the elbows out of the water. Remember to keep the elbows up and wrists relaxed. The hands then return to the starting position with the wrists low to the water. The follow-through of the head and

30

the downward kick of the legs enables the arms to return to the starting position. The hands enter simultaneously in front of the shoulders, finger tips first, getting ready to begin another stroke.

Breathing and Coordination

You will find that the breathing is a very important part of doing the butterfly stroke correctly.

The breath should be taken after you have exhaled under water by raising the head forward and jutting the chin outward. You should take the breath as the legs are in the downward beat of the kick and as the arms are moving through the push phase of the stroke. After the push phase of the stroke is complete, the head is then rolled forward and downward. The recovering arms at this time return to the starting position, preparing for the next stroke.

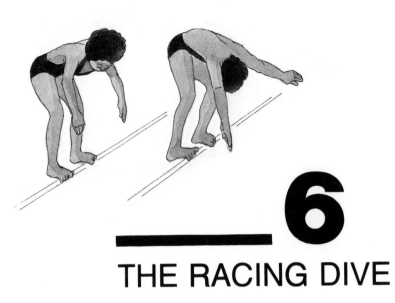

6

THE RACING DIVE

Now that we have pretty much mastered and understood the four competitive racing strokes, it is time to learn the correct and safe way of doing the racing dive.

Be sure you know the fundamentals of a proper and safe entry into a pool, ocean, lake, or pond. You should also be able to do a standing forward dive before undertaking the competitive start.

To begin the racing start we think it best to stand on the edge of the pool, with both feet shoulder-width apart, facing the water, with your toes curled over the edge.

From here the starting stance is then taken. Bend forward at the waist, slightly bending your knees. Your eyes should be looking down and forward, with your arms placed out in front of your body, hands down towards the water surface. Your feet are separated about shoulder width, your hands are usually placed just outside the feet. Each individual will have his or her own most comfortable position.

From this starting position the forward racing dive begins.

We have found that the movement is begun with the springing jump of the legs, and then a forward outstretched leap of the body over the water surface.

32

It is important that the first movement of the head and shoulders is down and not up. As the legs push the body forward, the arms take a wind-up swing to assist in throwing the body over the water.

As you are outstretched over the water surface, keep your head raised and looking forward. Directly prior to entry the head is then tucked between your outstretched arms. You should then try to slice the water, attempting to enter as streamline as possible.

After you make a streamline entry into the water, the swimming stroke is begun. The racing start which we just explained is used for all the strokes described, except for the backstroke.

The forward racing dive for butterfly, breaststroke and freestyle is done from a starting block located at the starting end of a competitive swimming pool. A starter during a swim meet would give you the following commands: "Swimmers Up!" . . . at which time you would stand up onto the starting block. Swimmers "Take your mark!" . . . at which time you would come down into a ready starting position. Then the gun or horn would sound . . . at which time you would begin your racing dive.

Alertness, fast reactions and good diving skills are very important for a quick, competitive start.

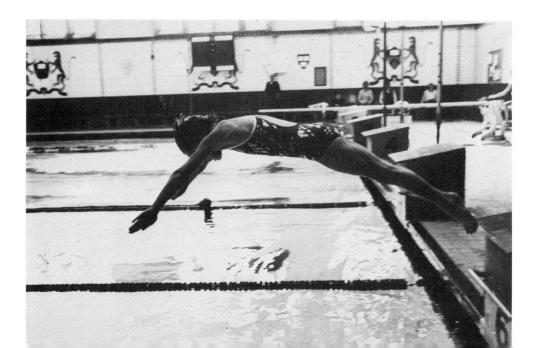

The Backstroke Start

The backstroke start is done with the swimmer in the water. You begin the backstroke from the same starting block from which the other dives were done. Placement of the toes on the wall is next. Specific swimming rules dictate whether or not your toes can go in the gutter of the pool. Be sure to learn all rules of all the strokes before you swim competitively.

After you place your toes, just about at the water level, you obtain a sure grip of the starting block backstroke handles.

When the starter gives you the command of "Take your mark," you then pull your body and your arms into a tight, tucked ball against the wall and starting block. At the sound of the gun or horn, you lift yourself upward and push yourself away from the starting block. Your head goes backward and your arms swing forward, up and over, extending above your head. As you press away from the wall, you try and clear the water, arching your back as you extend out.

Once the body is submerged, you bring yourself to the surface by tucking your chin to your chest and using one backstroke arm pull.

There are a lot of styles and forms of competitive racing dives. The starts we have just described are the most fundamental and easiest to learn. Other forms and styles should be taught by professional instructors or coaches.

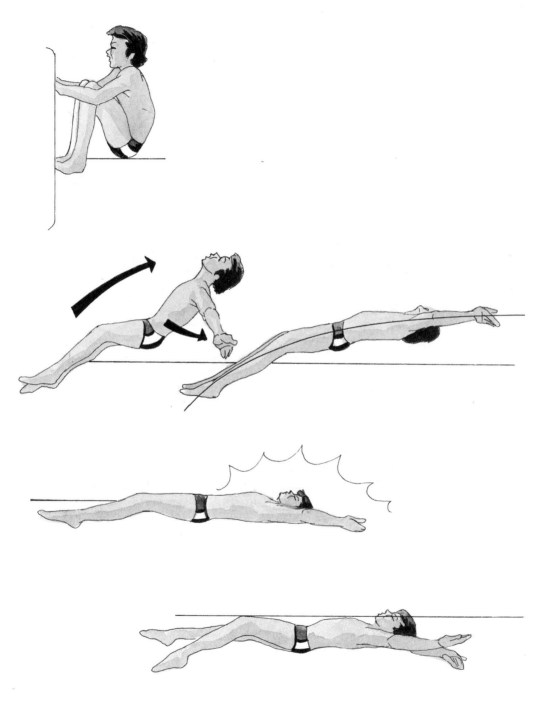

7

THE TURNS

More than likely, once you have learned the strokes, you might like to know how a swimmer can best make the turns.

Freestyle Open Turn

As the swimmer gets close to the end of the pool, one arm reaches out and pulls the head and body to the wall, leaning to the side of the outstretched arm. The free arm is at the side at the beginning of the turn and then hooks the water, helping to get the body into a tucked-ball position. When the body is tucked, it is time to rotate in the direction of the free arm. The final spin is made with the feet and tucked body pulling close into the wall .

The head and free arm lead the body off the wall. A breath is taken as the face clears the surface of the water. The turning arm is then put alongside the free arm, both pointing away from the wall. The head pops under the water between the

outstretched arms with the body under water and ready to push off. As the swimmer drives off the wall, extending from the tucked position, the arms must reach out into a full extension, allowing them to glide out and at a slight angle up to the water's surface. At the beginning of the pushoff, the swimmer blows air out under water. The glide lass until the body just begins to slow down, and then the legs should start kicking to get the swimmer moving on into the stroke.

If you decide to go into competitive swimming, you might like to learn another way of turning in freestyle, known as the "tumble" or "flip turn." With the faster "flip turn" a swimmer does not touch the wall with the hands; only the feet hit and push off.

Backstroke Turn

The rules tell us that when swimming backstroke, the swimmer must stay on his or her back until touching the end of the pool. As the turn is done, it is all right to roll off onto the side, but the push off must be done on the back.

Depending on which way the swimmer wants to turn, he will touch with one hand, palm flat against the wall, and thumb up. If turning to the right, the right hand touches the wall, rolling on the right as the elbow bends to bring the body closer into the wall.

The knees are tucked together up to the chest, and the body spins to the right toward the wall. The left arm pushes back and away against the water to speed up the spin. You keep on spinning until the feet are planted on the wall just below the surface of the water. The body at this point is crouched with the knees drawn up to the chest, and the hands are against the wall in front of the shoulders. Once a swimmer is able to do the above steps, the non-turning arm does not need to be brought to the

wall. It is used after the spin to begin the placement of head and shoulders in the water. At that moment, the swimmer takes a breath and the hips drop slightly, while the head and shoulders ease back into the water. The hands, palms up, still close to the wall, are carefully picked up to the shoulders with fingers leading. Then the hands, staying under the water, reach overhead.

The swimmer now pushes off from the wall with the arms fully extending. The body glides at a slight angle to the surface of the water, and the legs start kicking.

As soon as the head lies back in the water, the swimmer breathes out through the nose and continues until the face comes out of the water at the end of the glide.

Breaststroke and Butterfly Turns

In breaststroke and butterfly, the swimmer must touch the wall with both hands at the same level and at the same time. Then he or she can turn to the side, but during the push off, the hands must once again be on the chest.

The swimmer comes to the wall with both arms reaching out, grabbing the wall at the same time and at the same level. The elbows bend slightly, bringing the head and tucked body close to the wall. The head leads the body into the rotation, turning to the most comfortable side. The arms extend by pushing away from the wall and help to speed up the change of direction.

A breath is taken as the head is turned and the body is changing direction. As the head turns, the hand on the turning side will move away from the wall just alongside the head, finger tips first. As the body continues to turn, the other hand leaves the wall and goes alongside the other hand. At this point the elbows are slightly bent with the palms down.

The head should now be down between the arms and the body, in a crouched position, ready to push off as in the freestyle turn.

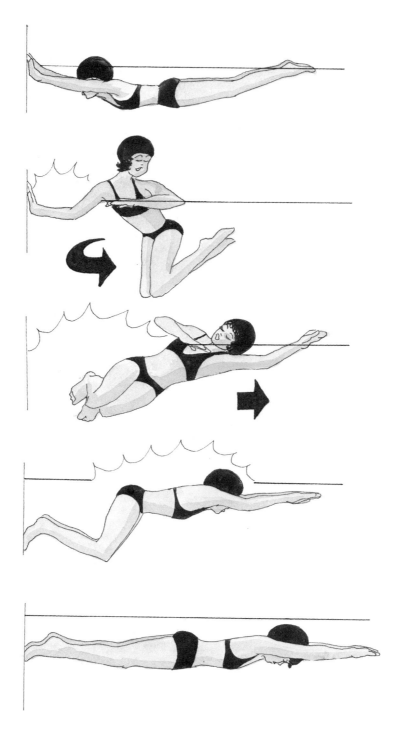

___8

HOW TO BE WATER SAFE

Everyone should know how to swim. Since more than 120,000,000 Americans participate in some form of recreational swimming or water activity, it is by far our nation's most popular sport. Therefore, it probably provides more opportunity by numbers alone for accidents to occur.

Being able to relax and remain at ease in the water is the mark of a good, safe swimmer. Safety means being safe and staying out of trouble. Being cautious and careful in all types of water makes for enjoyable and safe swimming and water activities.

Accidents around and in water can be dangerous and fatal. We cannot stress enough that you should know the hazards around pools, ponds, lakes and oceans. And, it is just as important to know how to handle accidents when and if they occur.

Be aware of the following:

Always know what the water conditions are. Water should always be felt before entering. Entry into unknown water can cause unexpected difficulties.

Always find out the depth of pools, ponds, lakes and oceans before you enter. The conditions of these areas should be known. Stay away from rocks, weeds or other underwater obstructions. Strong currents or rip tides should be avoided. If you ever get caught in a current, you should always remember to swim *parallel to shore*. *Do not panic* is the key thought to remember in all accident situations.

In every instance, *NEVER SWIM ALONE*. Swim in supervised areas, always following all the rules. Know your limitations, don't overestimate your ability, especially by using artificial swimming aids.

42

There is a system of safety which is used at a lot of swimming sites. This system is called the buddy system. What it involves are boys and girls swimming in pairs, always staying at a close distance to their partners. At any given time, a whistle or horn is sounded, at which time the two buddies raise their hands together, acknowledging that they are with one another and that both are safe. This method works well at lake-fronts and other large recreational areas.

Safety, in most instances, can be achieved by simply applying common sense. All of you know that you should not run on the deck of a pool, because it is usually very slippery and can cause accidents. Never call for help in the water unless you really need it—lifeguards strictly enforce this rule everywhere. Don't swim when you are extremely tired, overheated or directly after eating a large meal.

If you feel a cramp in your leg or stomach, relax, get to safety and knead the cramping muscle. Common sense should tell you not to swim when you are freezing cold, when you are sick, when you have a large open cut or sore on your skin, when you have an earache, when there is an electrical storm or, in general, when conditions don't permit safe swimming.

Out-of-doors over-exposure to the sun can result in a painful burn. Obviously, do not expose yourself to the sun more than a little bit (ten to twenty minutes at a time) in the beginning of the summer season until your body has built up some tanning protection.

Some people notice that after their first time in water a rash or irritation appears on their skin. Some find that their eyes or bodies react in a strange way to a chlorine-filled pool. Let your doctor check these allergic reactions to water.

Simple Rescues

In some emergencies, rescues can be done by almost anyone. This type of rescue is called a reaching rescue. The rescuer firmly plants his or her body onto the edge of the pool, pier or beach and extends a pole, towel or arm to aid the drowning victim, being extremely careful not to get pulled into the water. All rescues *must* be done without endangering the rescuer. Another common type of land rescue would be the ring buoy toss, in which the rescuer throws the victim a ring buoy with a rope attached and then pulls the subject to safety.

Both these rescues are done from land and should not endanger the rescuer if done correctly and with care. Other rescues and lifesaving techniques can be learned by enrolling in various water-safety courses available through the Red Cross. In addition to the simple reach and throw rescues, everyone can learn the methods of giving artificial respiration, whether they know how to swim or not. This is also taught in most first-aid and water-safety classes.

There are many water activities which you can pursue through proper certified teaching, such as lifesaving, scuba and skin diving, diving, water skiing, surfing, water polo and games, plus many more. These activities should only be attempted when you have proven that you are a good, safe, efficient swimmer. Always learn these other activities with proper qualified instruction.

Think Safe And Be Safe.

9

COMPETITIVE SWIMMING

You now may be asking yourself—how do I get to the Olympics? How do I win a ribbon or a medal? How fast can I really swim? All these things can happen by working hard, being dedicated and having patience.

If you can swim several laps of a 25-yard or 50-meter pool in several of the strokes that you just learned, then you may be ready to join a competitive swim team.

For swimmers just starting to swim competitively, no matter what age, there are a number of different ways to get started. There are summer leagues, park and recreation teams,

YMCA teams and clubs sponsored by and participating in the United States Swimming program.

The United States Swimming program, formerly a part of the Amateur Athletic Union, is set up in a progressive age group system allowing swimmers to swim against each other in their own age group. This system has been working very well for years, producing most of the Olympic, NCAA, AIAW, AAU and high school swimming stars.

Most all competitive swim meets are comprised of the following events. A medley relay of 400 yards involves four people swimming one of each of the four strokes for 100 yards each. The first swimmer starts with backstroke, the second swimmer goes breaststroke, the third goes butterfly and the last goes freestyle. Each swimmer starts the next leg of the relay just as the preceding swimmer finishes at the wall.

There usually is a freestyle relay in which all four swimmers go freestyle, starting in the same fashion as the medley relay.

Individual events are usually of two distances, a sprint of 50 and 100 yards or short event of 200 yards and a distance or long event of 500 yards or more. These individual events are in all four of the competitive strokes: backstroke, breaststroke, butterfly and freestyle.

There also are individual events, both short and long distances, which employ all four of the competitive strokes. They are called individual medleys. They are done by the swimmer going the first fourth of the race butterfly, the second quarter of the race backstroke, the third breaststroke and the last fourth freestyle.

All of these events offer the competitor a real challenge which can be very rewarding and gratifying to those who stick with it.

With coaching and experience on a swim team, you will learn how to swim each of your races. You can learn to negative split, descend, build up, and pace each event precisely to your talents and your needs. There are thousands of other things to be learned in your attempt to become a competitive swimmer. An

important element of learning is patience. Take the time and ability will come to you very easily.

Progressing through any swim program should make you both aquatically skilled and physically fit.

One of the best things about competitive swimming is what it has to offer the individual. You are given the opportunity to travel to new places, to meet people from different areas, often establishing very strong and lasting friendships. Then, of course, there is the thrill of racing against the clock—attempting to do even better than you had done before.

We both can only tell you that it was exciting and fun for us to swim competitively. In order to find out if you belong to the swimming crowd you will have to try it out for yourself.

Remember all great accomplishments start out the same way, by saying, "I'll try!"

INDEX